Restore the Joy:
Daily Devotions for December

Nancy J. Baker and Denise K. Loock

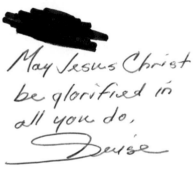

May Jesus Christ
be glorified in
all you do,
Denise

digdeeper
devotions

RESTORE THE JOY: DAILY DEVOTIONS FOR DECEMBER
BY NANCY J. BAKER and DENISE K. LOOCK
Published by Lightning Editing Services
699 Golf Course Rd., Waynesville, NC 28786

Copyright 2018 by Nancy J. Baker and Denise K. Loock

ISBN: 9781729474617

Cover and interior design by Lightning Editing Services

Available at amazon.com or digdeeperdevotions.com

For more information about this book and the authors, visit digdeeperdevotions.com.

Then the angel said to them,
"Do not be afraid,
for I bring you good tidings
of great joy
which will be to all people.
For there is born to you this day
in the city of David a Savior,
who is Christ the Lord."

Luke 2:10–11 NKJV

Table of Contents

December 1: Preparing a Path

John the Baptist said, *"Prepare the way for the Lord, make straight paths for him."* Matthew 3:3

The weekend after Thanksgiving means one thing for our family: prepare the house for Christmas. Over the years, we've discovered that decorating the house and yard before December 1 reduces stress during the rest of the holiday season. We prepare early so we can fully enjoy the festivities that follow.

In a similar way, we can prepare our hearts for Christmas, or as John the Baptist said, "Prepare the way for the Lord." The Greek word for "prepare," *hetoimazo*, comes from an ancient mid-eastern custom. Before a king took a journey, servants were sent ahead to remove any obstacles that might jeopardize the king's safety or his comfort. They leveled roads, removed stones, and scouted the area for robbers.[1]

John is quoting Isaiah when he exhorts his listeners to get ready for the Lord. Isaiah used the word *panah* for "prepare" (Isaiah 40:3). Under the Mosaic Law, if someone in a family became unclean through disease or illness, the whole house had to be thoroughly cleansed (Leviticus 14:36). *Panah* also means "to remove, to take out of the way" or "to put a house in order."[2]

Both *panah* and *hetoimazo* accurately describe my family's Christmas preparations. We move furniture around to make room for the tree, clear out the clutter, and then store unnecessary items in the basement.

I also need to clean my spiritual house—my heart. Paul gives instructions for heart scrubbing in Colossians 3. He says we should strip off our old evil nature and all its wicked deeds and dress ourselves in humility, gentleness, and patience (vv. 9,12).

After my spiritual makeover, I'm ready to celebrate the coming of King Jesus. And with Isaiah, I can rejoice because "the glory of the Lord [is] revealed, and all people will see it together" (Isaiah 40:5).

Are you preparing your heart for Christmas?

DIG DEEPER

1. Paul gives us a lot of instructions about "cleaning house" in Colossians 3:1–25. What other tasks does he suggest we perform?

2. John the Baptist described his duties as the path-preparer in John 1:19–28 and John 3:22–36. What was his attitude?

3. What does John the Baptist say about Jesus's identity in John 1:29–33? Why is he so sure about who Jesus is? Are you sure of Jesus's identity? Read Jesus's description of himself in John 5:19–29.

December 2: A Message of Hope

Your throne, O God, will last for ever and ever; a scepter of justice will be the scepter of your kingdom. You love righteousness and hate wickedness; therefore God, your God, has set you above your companions by anointing you with the oil of joy. Psalm 45:6–7

One of the earliest prophecies proclaiming the birth of Christ occurs in Genesis 49:10 when Jacob blessed each of his sons. To Judah he said, "The scepter will not depart from Judah, nor the ruler's staff from between his feet until he to whom it belongs shall come, and the obedience of the nations shall be his."

Judah and his brothers must have thought that was a strange thing to say. They had no kingdom to rule. They didn't even have a country anymore. Due to a famine, they were refugees in Egypt, dependent on the charity of Pharaoh.

No doubt Jacob's sons knew about the covenant God had made with their great-grandfather Abraham. Jacob had surely told them what God had said to Abraham: 'I will make you into a great nation, and I will bless you. ... and all peoples on earth will be blessed through you" (Genesis 12:2–3). But that promise must have seemed like an old man's fantasy to the eleven brothers as they tended Pharaoh's flocks in Goshen.

Nevertheless, God kept his promise and Jacob's words came true. Judah's descendants, David and Solomon, reigned over many people. However, the "ruler's staff" Jacob mentioned belongs to only one individual because

5

only one king will command the obedience of all nations—Jesus Christ.

God's promises may seem a little far-fetched to you this Christmas season. Maybe you're grieving the death of a loved one or the end of a cherished relationship. Maybe you've lost your job, and you lie awake at night wondering how to pay the bills. Maybe a family crisis has left you thinking that God has blocked your calls.

But into our crises, God sends messages of hope. He delivered a promise to Jacob's sons in Egypt: The Scepter of Justice is coming. Better days are ahead. He delivers a similar promise to us: The day is coming when the kingdoms of the world will "become the kingdom of our Lord and of his Messiah, and he will reign forever and ever" (Revelation 11:15).

Will you rejoice this Christmas as you look forward to that day?

DIG DEEPER

1. In some translations, Genesis 49:10 reads "until Shiloh come" instead of "until he to whom it belongs shall come" Many Bible scholars believe that Shiloh means "peacemaker" and therefore is another word for Messiah. How was the Messiah a peacemaker? Read Luke 2:14 and Ephesians 2:11–22.

2. Read Psalm 45. What verses make clear that the psalmist is writing about Jesus and not just a human king?

3. Psalm 45:6–7 is quoted in Hebrews 1:8–9. Read all of Hebrews 1. Why is Jesus superior to any other being in heaven and on earth?

4. When we arrive in heaven, what will our place in Jesus's kingdom be? Read 2 Timothy 2:12 and Revelation 20:6.

December 3: Conversing with Angels

Your promises have been thoroughly tested, and your servant loves them. Psalm 119:140

When the angel Gabriel told Zechariah that his barren, elderly wife, Elizabeth, was going to bear a child, Zechariah replied, "How can I be sure of this?" (Luke 1:18).

I chuckled when I read that. An angel was talking to Zechariah. Gabriel had materialized in the temple next to the altar of incense just like a character in *Star Trek*. Zechariah was "gripped with fear" when Gabriel appeared, but then he was cheeky enough to ask, "Are you sure?"

Gabriel's answer indicated that he was a little surprised by Zechariah's doubt. "I am Gabriel," he said. "I stand in the presence of God" (v. 19). In other words, Gabriel was saying, "Are you nuts? I'm an archangel of the Most High God! Who do you think sent me here to tell you this? Of course I'm sure."

I'd like to think that if an angel appeared before me with a message from God, I'd believe him without hesitation. But Zechariah's experience suggests I probably wouldn't, especially if the message was as stunning as Gabriel's was.

God disciplined Zechariah for his unbelief by taking away his ability to speak until the promised child was born (v. 20). God may also discipline me when I don't respond to his promises in faith. God assures us that every word in the Scriptures is true (2 Timothy 3:16). He also says that every word that comes from his mouth will accomplish what he desires and achieve the purpose for which he sends it (Isaiah 55:10–11).

I may never have the privilege of conversing with an angel here on earth, but I can receive a message from God at any time and in any place if I open my Bible with a hearing heart and wait for him to speak.

Are you ready to listen to whatever message God may want to deliver to you today?

DIG DEEPER

1. Read Luke 1:67–79. When God restored Zechariah's speech, what did Zechariah say? Why was his heart so full of praise?

2. Gabriel appeared to at least two other people in the Bible. How did they react? Read Daniel 8:15–19 and Luke 1:26–38.

3. Read John 12:44–50. What did Jesus say about people who don't believe his words?

December 4: The Perfect Leader

For to us a child is born, to us a son is given, and the government will be on his shoulders. Isaiah 9:6

We want to change the government. We want to elect a leader who'll do what is good for the people, who'll serve them rather than himself. Someone who inspires and encourages rather than one with empty promises. Someone who is both strong and decisive, but also compassionate. Someone who understands our problems and brings us hope for the future. Someone who will establish a perfect society with justice for all.

Can we find such a person?

God promised such a leader through his prophet Isaiah. Sprinkled throughout several chapters in Isaiah (42, 49, 50, and 52–53) are four songs that describe a servant leader. This world leader has the greatest endorsement anyone can have: God's! "Here is my servant, whom I uphold, my chosen one in whom I delight; I will put my Spirit on him, and he will bring justice to the nations (Isaiah 42:1).

This leader serves God and others, not himself. He is compassionate; he understands our weaknesses and problems. "A bruised reed he will not break, and a smoldering wick he will not snuff out" (Isaiah 42:3). Ever feel bruised? About to be snuffed out?

This leader may appear weak. He seems to lack political ambition. "He will not shout or cry out, or raise his voice in the streets" (Isaiah 42:2). He looks pretty ordinary. "He had no beauty or majesty to attract us to him, nothing in his

13

appearance that we should desire him" (Isaiah 53:2). We often prefer tall and handsome men like King Saul (1 Samuel 9:2 and 10:18–23).

God promised that his servant "will be raised and lifted up and highly exalted" (Isaiah 52:13). He will rule over all the earth. We will not be disappointed. He keeps his promises.

Does this leader get your vote? Are you excited about the new government that's coming someday?

DIG DEEPER

1. Read Psalm 2:1–12. From where will God's ruler reign? What are God's promises and warnings concerning him? What is his relationship to God?

2. Read 2 Thessalonians 2:1–10. Before Jesus Christ, God's servant, comes to set up his government on earth, an imposter will rise up as a world leader. By whom is he endorsed? (See verse 9.) How is he described? Why do people follow him even though he's evil? How is he overcome?

3. Read the four servant songs recorded in Isaiah 42:1–9, 49:1–13, 50:4–9 and 52:13–53:12. List other characteristics of God's servant leader.

December 5: We Three Kings of Judah

Of the greatness of his government and peace there will be no end. He will reign on David's throne and over his kingdom, establishing and upholding it with justice and righteousness from that time on and forever. The zeal of the Lord Almighty will accomplish this. Isaiah 9:7

Reading about the kings who descended from David, we might shake our heads and say, "Surely the Forever King will not come from this bunch!" Few of Israel's kings were exemplary; most weren't people we'd want to claim as relatives, much less our rulers. Some, like Solomon, began well but finished far from God (1 Kings 11:3–10).

Solomon's corrupt lifestyle probably had a negative influence on his son Rehoboam. When he became king, Rehoboam chose to listen to his peers, not his people. "My father laid on you a heavy yoke; I will make it even heavier," he told them. "My father scourged you with whips; I will scourge you with scorpions" (1 Kings 12:11).

As a result, most of the tribes of Israel rebelled and crowned their own king, Jeroboam, who was not of David's line. Only Judah and part of Benjamin remained loyal to Rehoboam. Under his rule, the people indulged in wickedness: "By the sins they committed they stirred up [God's] jealous anger more than those who were before them had done" (1 Kings 14:22).

Rehoboam's son, Abijah, reigned only three years. He committed all the sins of his father. In contrast, Abijah's son Asa reigned forty-one years. He did what was right in the eyes of the Lord as David had done and his heart was fully committed to the Lord all his life (1Kings 15:9–14). He even deposed his grandmother, the queen mother, because she made a pole for Asherah.[3]

God preserved the line of David in spite of their idolatry and disobedience: "Nevertheless, for David's sake the Lord his God gave [Abijah and the other kings] a lamp in Jerusalem by raising up [sons to succeed them] and by making Jerusalem strong (1Kings 15:4–5).

God not only makes promises, he zealously accomplishes them. Hundreds of years after God's promise to David (1 Chronicles 17:11–14), Joseph went to Bethlehem because he belonged to the line of David (Luke 2:4).

Aren't you glad that God keeps his promises—in spite of the sins of his people?

DIG DEEPER

1. The book of Judges ends with this sad statement: "everyone did as they saw fit" (21:25). We read a similar rebellious refrain in the biographies of the kings. What were the things David did that other leaders should follow? See 1 Kings 14:7–8; 15:9–14.

2. Compare David's experiences as expressed in Psalm 69:7–9 to those Jesus experienced while he was on earth. What does verse 9 mean by "zeal for [God's] house"? (Hint: not a literal building). Are you zealous for God's house?

3. God is sovereign over history. Joseph and Mary lived in Nazareth, but God had told the prophets that the Messiah would be born in Bethlehem. How did God arrange the place of Jesus' birth? How did God arrange two other prophecies related to Jesus's childhood as recorded in Matthew 2:1–23? Can you see signs of God's sovereignty over your own history?

December 6: Anticipation

The shepherds said to one another, "Let's go to Bethlehem and see this thing that has happened" ... so they hurried off and found Mary and Joseph, and the baby, who was lying in a manger. Luke 2:15–16

Okay. I admit it. As soon as I hear the word *anticipation*, I start humming a few bars of Carly Simon's 1971 mega-hit. And yes, the image of a slightly tilted Heinz ketchup bottle flashes across my mind's monitor. (I'm that old.) Surprisingly, the pop tune and the commercial for my favorite condiment have more in common with the concept of biblical anticipation than I first thought.

The word *anticipation* doesn't appear in the KJV or NIV translations of the Bible. However, the NASB translators used "anticipation" once, in Psalm 119:148, for the Hebrew word *qadam*, which means "to come to meet" or "to go before."[4] *Qadam* is used often in the book of Psalms; usually, though, it is translated "come." For example, Asaph used it when he prayed, "May your mercy come quickly to meet us" (Psalm 79:8).

"Come quickly" reminds me of an Old Testament story. Joseph jumped into his chariot and rushed to meet his father's caravan in Genesis 46:29. In the New Testament, the prodigal son's father saw his son coming and ran to greet him (Luke 15:20). These two incidents illustrate biblical anticipation—the can't-wait aspect of our faith. Joseph and the prodigal son's father rushed to a reunion with loved ones they already knew intimately. They hurried

21

toward their loved ones because they couldn't wait to reestablish a relationship with them.

In Luke 2:15–16, the shepherds "made haste" to Bethlehem (KJV). The Greek word for "haste" is *speudo*, which can be translated "to desire earnestly."[5] Nothing was going to prevent the shepherds from establishing a relationship with the newborn king.

God earnestly desires that we spend time with him this Christmas. Are we rushing to see him?

DIG DEEPER

1. In Psalm 95:1–6, *qadam* is translated "come." According to this passage, what should we rush to do and why should we rush to do it?

2. As post-resurrection Christians, we also participate in another kind of anticipation. Read 2 Peter 3:10–12. What is he encouraging believers to do? (Note: the word *speudo* is used in verse 12.)

3. Getting together with families during the holidays can be stressful. Read the prodigal son's story in Luke 15:11–32. What can we learn from the father's example about dealing with family conflicts?

December 7: Good Tidings of Great Joy

I will greatly rejoice in the Lord, my soul shall be joyful in my God; for he hath clothed me with the garments of salvation, he hath covered me with the robe of righteousness. Isaiah 61:10 (KJV)

"Fear not: for, behold, I bring you good tidings of great joy," the angel told the shepherds on the night of Jesus's birth. What were those tidings? "For unto you is born this day in the city of David a Savior, which is Christ the Lord" (Luke 2:10–11 KJV).

The angel's message brought great joy to the shepherds because the Jewish people had been waiting for the birth of the Messiah for centuries. Isaiah, and many other prophets, had promised that God would send a mighty Redeemer, the Holy One of Jacob, who would defeat Israel's enemies and establish a glorious kingdom (Isaiah 47:4; 49:7).

When the shepherds arrived at the stable, I wonder if Mary and Joseph shared with them what the angel had told Joseph: "Give him the name Jesus, because he will save his people from their sins" (Matthew 1:21). Was that the message of joy the shepherds spread abroad the night of Jesus's birth? Or did they glorify and praise God simply because they thought that the rule of their Roman oppressors would soon end?

What joy fills your heart this Christmas? Our joy encompasses more than the Savior's birth, his past ministry on earth, and his future reign as King of Kings. It also refers to the joy that no one can take away from us (John 16:22). This joy, Jesus said, is available to us right now if we abide within the boundaries of his love and obey his commandments (John 15:9–11).

The exuberant lyrics of "How Great Our Joy" celebrate the everlasting joy we experience when we understand the completeness of the salvation our Savior, Christ the Lord, provides for us:

> This gift of God we'll cherish well,
> That ever joy our hearts shall fill.
> How great our joy! Great our joy!
> Joy, joy, joy! Joy, joy, joy!
> Praise we the Lord in heaven on high!

The source of our joy is a person; the fullness of our joy is measured by the intimacy of our relationship with him. The more time we spend in his presence, through prayer and Bible study, the more joy we will experience.

How full is your joy?

DIG DEEPER

1. Read Psalm 16. Why is the psalmist filled with joy? In verse 9, he gives an intriguing description of joy—"my flesh also shall rest in hope" (KJV). What does that phrase signify to you?

2. Read John 16:16–33. On the eve of his death, what did Jesus tell the disciples about joy? Which of the promises Jesus gave the disciples comforts you the most in your present circumstances?

3. Chapters 35, 51, and 61 in Isaiah are messages of encouragement. Take time to read them this week. Choose one promise from each chapter and thank God for his faithfulness.

"How Great Our Joy"

Traditional German carol
Translated into English by Theodore Baker
Public Domain

While by the sheep we watched at night,
Glad tidings brought an angel bright.

Refrain:
How great our joy! Great our joy!
Joy, joy, joy! Joy, joy, joy!
Praise we the Lord in heaven on high!
Praise we the Lord in heaven on high!

There shall be born, so He did say,
In Bethlehem a Child today.

There shall the Child lie in a stall,
This Child who shall redeem us all.

This gift of God we'll cherish well,
That ever joy our hearts shall fill.

December 8: An Everlasting Gift

God says, *"Incline you ear, and come to Me. Hear, and your soul shall live; and I will make an everlasting covenant with you—the sure mercies of David."* Isaiah 55:3 (NKJV)

I've received many Christmas gifts. Some gifts, like the cassette tape player I wanted so desperately in 1971, were discarded long ago.

Other gifts I'll cherish my whole life, like the tiny crystal bird from my mom and the ornaments my children made in preschool. Someday, however, even these treasured gifts may be lost or broken; they will not last forever.

Isaiah reminded his listeners of an everlasting gift, one that could never be lost or broken. He spoke of God's everlasting covenant that he called "the sure mercies of David." God had promised David, "I will raise up your offspring to succeed you ... and I will establish the throne of his kingdom forever. ... I will be his father, and he shall be my son. ... and my love will never be taken away from him" (2 Samuel 7:12–15).

Historically, David's heir was Solomon, but his kingdom, as magnificent as it was, endured only forty years. Spiritually, God was speaking of another heir to David's throne—Jesus, who will reign forever (Luke 1:32–33).

The people of Isaiah's day needed to hear his message of hope because the Babylonians were going to invade Israel and destroy Jerusalem. During the seventy years of captivity that followed, God's people needed the assurance that God had not abandoned them forever.

During difficult times we need to be reminded of God's "sure mercies" too. In the apostle Paul's sermon at Antioch, he declared that post-resurrection Christians are the spiritual offspring of David (see Acts 13:32–34). Therefore, the everlasting covenantal promises given to David and to the nation of Israel apply to us as well.

What are the "sure mercies" of God's eternal covenant? Isaiah referred to many of them: God graciously gives us everlasting strength (26:4 KJV), everlasting joy (61:7), everlasting kindness (54:8), and an everlasting name (56:5). His everlasting salvation provides everlasting light (45:17; 60:19–20).

These gifts will never lose their value and can never be lost or broken. Are you enjoying the everlasting gifts that your Everlasting Father has given you?

DIG DEEPER

1. Read Paul's sermon in Acts 13:16–41. To whom is Paul speaking? (vv. 16, 26). What is the main point of his message?

2. Read the benediction in Hebrews 13:20–21. To what everlasting covenant is the writer referring? What are the benefits of that covenant according to verse 21?

3. Read 2 Samuel 7:8–16. What benefits of that covenant apply to us? What parts of it refer specifically to Jesus?

December 9: Prophetic Fulfillment

For the Lord God does nothing without revealing his secret to his servants the prophets. The lion has roared; who will not fear? The Lord God has spoken; who can but prophesy? Amos 3:7–8 (ESV)

My husband and I once climbed a small mountain. At the top, we saw both where we had come from and down the other side. How different our mountaintop experience would've been if a helicopter had simply placed us there. We would've still seen the wonderful vista, but we would've missed the rocks and the stream along the twisty trail we'd climbed.

I thought of that climb when I finished reading the Old Testament and began to read the New Testament, I felt like I was on top of a mountain with two views. Having recently read through the Prophets, I imagined Matthew's excitement when he wrote that "all this took place to fulfill what the Lord had said through the prophet: 'The virgin will conceive and give birth to a son, and they will call him Immanuel (which means 'God with us')'" (Matthew 1:22–23 quoting Isaiah 7:14).

Hundreds of years after Isaiah died, his prophecy was fulfilled through Mary and Joseph. They were engaged but did not have sexual relations until after she gave birth to a son conceived by the Holy Spirit (Matthew 1:18, 24–25). God gave over 100 other prophecies in the Old Testament foretelling the birth, ministry, and death of Jesus. The gospels record the fulfillment of all those prophecies.

Why had God given those prophecies? The prophets lived in times of political upheaval, natural disasters, and failed leadership. The people rebelled and didn't want God telling them what to do. They said, "Do not prophesy to us what is right; speak to us smooth things, prophesy illusions, leave the way, turn aside from the path, let us hear no more about the Holy One of Israel" (Isaiah 30:10–11 ESV).

But the prophets faithfully proclaimed God's words. Those who listened and believed were encouraged. They knew that no matter how bad things became, God had a plan. In the prophecies, they saw God's sovereignty and his faithfulness. One day he would send a child who would save them from their sins.

When we read the Bible, we stand on a mountaintop looking at both the past and the future of God's people. Do you see God's plan in his Word as it unfolded in the past and as it promises to unfold in the future?

DIG DEEPER

1. The people not only refused to hear God's prophets, they appointed false ones who would tell them what they wanted to hear. Read Amos 8:11–12. How did God respond? When did he break the silence? See Luke 1:5–25, 57-80.

2. Read Luke 4:16–30. How did the people react when Jesus claimed he fulfilled the prophecy in Isaiah 61:1–2? (Note that he purposely stopped reading before he came to "the day of vengeance" in verse 2, which refers to his second coming.) What was Jesus claiming? Why couldn't they believe him?

3. Read Isaiah 1:1–20. As you compare the times of the prophets to our own times, what similarities and differences do you see? What do you know of God's plan for the end of the age in which we live? Does his plan for Jesus to return as conqueror and judge frighten or reassure you?

December 10: Radiance of God's Mercy

Who is a God like you, who pardons sin and forgives the transgression of the remnant of his inheritance? You do not stay angry forever but delight to show mercy. Micah 7:18

"It was the best of times; it was the worst of times."[6] So wrote Charles Dickens about the late eighteenth century. The prophet Micah could have described his era the same way. He lived during the reigns of two godly kings, Jotham and Hezekiah, and one ungodly king, Ahaz.

Although Judah's citizens enjoyed years of prosperity under Hezekiah, God declared that the nation's spiritual health was "beyond all remedy" (Micah 2:10). From his holy temple, God saw the sins of his people and announced that they would be disciplined (1:2–16).

But—and thankfully there is always a *but* in our merciful God's vocabulary—he also promised to redeem them (4:10). Out of the village of Bethlehem, a ruler would come; he would bring peace, and his greatness would reach the ends of the earth (5:2–5).

That magnificent promise filled Micah's heart with confidence. He determined to "watch in hope" for the Lord's deliverance. The darkness of sin wouldn't drive him into a cave of despair. In faith he declared, "Though I sit in darkness, the Lord will be my light . . . He will bring me out into the light; and I will see his righteousness" (7:7–9).

Sometimes darkness seems impenetrable. The thick curtain of national or personal wrongdoing can block the light of God's sovereignty and righteousness. Broken relationships,

39

unethical choices, or financial folly can imprison us in pitch-black gloom.

But we don't have to remain there. Two thousand years ago, God sent the Everlasting Light of salvation to Bethlehem. And nothing can extinguish the brilliance of the grace and mercy Jesus Christ brought into the world. Because he came and died for us, we can walk in perpetual light (1 John 1:5–7). With Micah we can rejoice, "You will again have compassion on us; you will tread our sins underfoot and hurl all our iniquities into the depths of the sea" (Micah 7:19).

Do you feel as if you're engulfed in darkness? Ask God to send the light of his eternal love and the radiance of his unending mercy to dispel whatever darkness currently shadows your life.

DIG DEEPER

1. Micah and Isaiah were contemporaries. Compare Micah 7:7–20 with Isaiah 60:1–22. What similarities do you see? In what ways do their words encourage you?

2. The Jews of Jesus's day were expecting a conquering Messiah. Read Micah 4:1–8 and 11–13. How do these verses describe the coming ruler and his kingdom? Can you see why even Jesus's disciples were confused?

3. The Hebrew word translated *hope* in Micah 7:7 means "to expect, to wait for."[7] What should we be expecting? Read Psalm 27:13–14 and Titus 2:13.

December 11: Feeling Insignificant?

But you, Bethlehem, in the land of Judah, are by no means least among the rulers of Judah; for out of you will come a ruler who will shepherd my people Israel. Matthew 2:6

As a child, I grew older but not much taller. Even my younger brother passed me in height. I was called "the runt of the litter" or "Shorty" and other nicknames that made me feel insignificant in comparison to the taller members of my family.

In the Old Testament, God sent a prophet named Samuel to Bethlehem to anoint a king from among Jesse's sons. Samuel was impressed by each of the seven sons who passed before him, but God had not chosen any of them.

God said, "Do not look on his appearance or on the height of his stature, because I have rejected him. For the Lord sees not as man sees: man looks on the outward appearance, but the Lord looks on the heart" (1 Samuel 16:7 ESV). When the youngest came, God said, "David is the one."

Centuries later, a census required a young virgin named Mary and her espoused husband to go to Bethlehem because both were of the lineage of David. They arrived just as she was about to give birth. Angels silently gathered and kept "their watch of wondering love." They knew that months earlier God had sent the angel Gabriel to tell Mary she would conceive by the Holy Spirit and give birth to the Messiah, the Christ.

When Jesus was born, the angels' voices filled the night and "everlasting light" shone in the dark streets. That night's events in Bethlehem would be sung for centuries to come.

In the well-known carol "O Little Town of Bethlehem," the word *little* may suggest that Bethlehem was an insignificant village. But God chose Bethlehem from among thousands of towns in Judah.

We may feel small and unimportant too. But God values each of us and chose to send his Son to redeem us.

> O holy Child of Bethlehem
> Descend to us, we pray
> Cast out our sin and enter in
> Be born in us today
> We hear the Christmas angels
> The great glad tidings tell
> O come to us, abide with us
> O Lord Emmanuel.

Is that your prayer this Christmas?

DIG DEEPER

1. According to 1 Corinthians 1:27–31, who does God choose and why does he choose them?

2. How does Jesus treat a man who was short—"little in stature" (KJV) as recorded in Luke 19:1–10? Did you sing about this "wee little man" in Sunday school?

3. Read Ruth 4:11–15. Do you see a picture of Jesus in the blessings the elders and women of Bethlehem speak over Boaz, Ruth, and Naomi?

"O Little Town of Bethlehem"

Phillips Brooks, 1867
Public Domain

O little town of Bethlehem,
how still we see thee lie!
Above thy deep and dreamless sleep
the silent stars go by.
Yet in thy dark streets shineth
the everlasting Light;
The hopes and fears of all the years
are met in thee tonight.

For Christ is born of Mary,
and gathered all above,
While mortals sleep, the angels keep
their watch of wondering love.
O morning stars together,
proclaim the holy birth,
And praises sing to God the King,
and peace to men on earth!

How silently, how silently,
the wondrous Gift is giv'n;
So God imparts to human hearts
 the blessings of His Heav'n.
No ear may hear His coming,
but in this world of sin,
Where meek souls will receive Him still,
the dear Christ enters in.

Where children pure and happy pray
to the blessèd Child,
Where misery cries out to Thee,
Son of the mother mild;
Where charity stands watching

and faith holds wide the door,
The dark night wakes, the glory breaks,
and Christmas comes once more.

O holy Child of Bethlehem,
descend to us, we pray;
Cast out our sin, and enter in,
be born in us today.
We hear the Christmas angels
the great glad tidings tell;
O come to us, abide with us,
our Lord Emmanuel!

December 12: Promise-Bearers

"I will make you like my signet ring, for I have chosen you," declares the Lord Almighty. Haggai 2:23

Busyness isn't always productive, especially in spiritual matters. With eagerness and joy, the Jews who had returned from Babylon rebuilt the temple's foundation (Ezra 3:6–13). However, soon they became busy with other activities—rebuilding their homes, planting their fields, earning a living. The work on the temple stopped for at least fifteen years.

God then sent the prophet Haggai to Jerusalem. Over a four-month period he delivered four messages to Zerubbabel, the governor, and the Jews living in Jerusalem. What was Haggai's first message? Be convicted. You are neglecting God's work (Haggai 1:1–15). The people listened and obeyed.

Two months later, Haggai delivered another message: Be strong—courageous and comforted. God is with you (2:1–9). The people had become discouraged because the new temple wasn't as glorious as Solomon's temple had been. God reminded them that his presence made the temple glorious and his blessing made it a place of peace.

Two more months passed. Haggai received a message for the priests: Be clean. You're trying to do God's work without maintaining personal holiness (2:10–19). Apparently they had forgotten that God valued holiness over busyness.

Finally, God sent a message for Zerubbabel, but its promise was relevant to all the Jews and to us: Be confident. God keeps his promises (2:20–23). Zerubbabel was the grandson of King Jehoiachin, a descendant of David. Zerubbabel would never sit on a throne, but one of his descendants, Jesus, would reclaim David's throne, and he would reign forever. God called Zerubbabel his "signet ring"—a symbol of royal authority, proof that God would fulfill his promise to David.

God has also chosen us to represent him. As his signet rings, we are authorized to proclaim the certainty of his promise—the Messiah is coming again. But we can't speak that message authoritatively unless we speak it authentically.

Meditate on Haggai's first three messages: Are we doing God's work? Do we work with confidence and courage, knowing God is with us? Are we pursuing personal holiness?

Let's not confuse busyness with spiritual growth or equate activity with obedience. Let's be the workers and representatives God has designed us to be. How can you step away from the busyness of the Christmas season to share the message of the Messiah with someone?

DIG DEEPER

1. Read Haggai 2. Circle each "I will" promise God makes. Which of those promises are most meaningful to you?

2. Compare Haggai's prophecy in 2:6–9 with Revelation 21:3-7. How should we prepare for the glorious day when peace on earth becomes a reality? Read Titus 2:11–14.

3. Zerubbabel's name appears in both of Jesus's genealogies (Matthew 1:12 and Luke 3:27). What other names appear in both genealogies?

4. Charles Wesley referred to Haggai 2:7 in "Hark! the Herald Angels Sing" when he wrote "Come, Desire of Nations, Come."[8] See the other names of Jesus that Wesley used in this beloved Christmas hymn on the following page.

"Hark! The Herald Angels Sing"

Charles Wesley, 1739*
Public Domain

Hark, how all the welkin rings,
"Glory to the King of kings;
Peace on earth, and mercy mild,
God and sinners reconciled!"
Joyful, all ye nations, rise,
Join the triumph of the skies;
Universal nature say,
"Christ the Lord is born to-day!"

Christ, by highest Heaven ador'd,
Christ, the everlasting Lord:
Late in time behold him come,
Offspring of a Virgin's womb!
Veiled in flesh, the Godhead see,
Hail the incarnate deity!
Pleased as man with men to appear,
Jesus! Our Immanuel here!

Hail, the heavenly Prince of Peace!
Hail, the Sun of Righteousness!
Light and life to all he brings,
Risen with healing in his wings.
Mild He lays his glory by,
Born that man no more may die;
Born to raise the sons of earth;
Born to give them second birth.

Come, Desire of nations, come,
Fix in us thy humble home;
Rise, the woman's conquering seed,
Bruise in us the serpent's head.
Now display thy saving power,
Ruined nature now restore;

Now in mystic union join
Thine to ours, and ours to thine.

Adam's likeness, Lord, efface;
Stamp Thy image in its place.
Second Adam from above,
Reinstate us in thy love.
Let us Thee, though lost, regain,
Thee, the life, the inner Man:
O! to all thyself impart,
Form'd in each believing heart.

*Wesley's original lyrics differ slightly from the more familiar lyrics that appear in modern hymnals.

December 13: A Welcoming Heart

For this is what the high and exalted One says— he who lives forever, whose name is holy: "I live in a high and holy place, but also with the one who is contrite and lowly in spirit, to revive the spirit of the lowly and to revive the heart of the contrite. Isaiah 57:15

Some congregations today omit hymns like "Thou Didst Leave Thy Throne and Thy Kingly Crown" (1864) because of its outdated language. But they lose much. Emily Elliott's hymn bursts with inspired images of the life of Jesus Christ—before, during, and after his incarnation.

Elliott begins before the nativity and pictures the Lord Jesus taking off his crown and putting it aside. He then descends from his heavenly throne to Bethlehem in the form of a baby.

Unfortunately, the tiny town is overcrowded with travelers and there is no room in the inn for his parents, Mary and Joseph. The baby is born in a stable (Luke 2:7).

Each of the hymn's first four stanzas ends with the refrain:

> O come to my heart, Lord Jesus,
> There is room in my heart for Thee.

Elliott also depicts Jesus's ministry. He did not choose to live in a mansion or palace. He was in effect a homeless man (see Matthew 8:20):

> The foxes found rest,
> and the birds their nest
> In the shade of the forest tree;
> But Thy couch was the sod,

> O Thou Son of God,
> In the deserts of Galilee.

We can hear the hymn writer's grief as she describes how most people had no room in their hearts for him during his years of ministry:

> Thou camest, O Lord,
> with the living word
> That should set Thy people free;
> But with mocking scorn,
> and with crown of thorn,
> They bore Thee to Calvary.

However, Elliott's biography doesn't end here. She jumps forward to Jesus's second coming in victory to gather his people to himself (Matthew 24:31):

> When the heav'ns shall ring,
> and her choirs sing,
> At Thy coming to victory,
> Let Thy voice call me home,
> saying, "Yet there is room,"
> There is room at My side for thee."
> My heart shall rejoice, Lord Jesus,
> When Thou comest and callest for me.

Make room in your heart this Christmas for the Lord Jesus and his living Word.

DIG DEEPER

1. Read Philippians 2:1–8. How did Christ exhibit the qualities of humility, serving, and obedience? How can you follow his example?

2. Elliot speaks of the "mocking scorn" Jesus endured in her hymn. Read Luke 23:32–43. Who mocked Jesus when during his crucifixion? How did Jesus respond to them? How do you respond when you're mocked because of your faith?

3. When Christ comes in victory, who will be at his side according to 1 Thessalonians 4:16–18? Will he be calling to you with his "loud command"?

"Thou Didst Leave Thy Throne"

Emily Elliott, 1864
Public Domain

Thou didst leave Thy throne
 and Thy kingly crown,
When Thou camest to earth for me;
But in Bethlehem's home
was there found no room
For Thy holy nativity.

Refrain:
O come to my heart, Lord Jesus,
There is room in my heart for Thee.

Heaven's arches rang when the angels sang,
Proclaiming Thy royal degree;
But of lowly birth didst Thou come to earth,
And in great humility.

The foxes found rest,
and the birds their nest
In the shade of the forest tree;
But Thy couch was the sod,
O Thou Son of God,
In the deserts of Galilee.

Thou camest, O Lord, with the living Word,
That should set Thy people free;
But with mocking scorn
and with crown of thorn,
They bore Thee to Calvary.

When the heav'ns shall ring,
and her choirs shall sing,
At Thy coming to victory,
Let Thy voice call me home,

saying "Yet there is room,
There is room at My side for thee."

Final Refrain:
My heart shall rejoice, Lord Jesus,
When Thou comest and callest for me.

December 14: God's Christmas Message

"For I am a great king," says the Lord Almighty, "and my name is to be feared among the nations." Malachi 1:14

Bills, advertisements, and credit card offers—the contents of my mailbox on most days. But during December, I receive the welcome addition of cards and newsy letters from friends and family. Their updates let me know what's important to them—their activities, goals, challenges, and blessings.

Unfortunately, God doesn't send updates through the postal service. For centuries, however, he delivered messages through prophets such as Malachi. His book contains a series of messages that help us understand what is important to God.

First God said, "I have loved you" (1:2). His people, however, hadn't loved him in return. They hadn't honored his name—shown him respect and worshiped him properly. Instead they'd given him unacceptable offerings and blasphemous insults (1:11–14).

God then reminded the priests of the covenant of life and peace he had made with them (Numbers 25:10–13). They had disregarded the covenant (Malachi 2:1–9). The people were also unfaithful, ignoring God's laws about sacrifices, marriage, and tithing (2:11–17; 3:8–15).

Nevertheless, in spite of their faithlessness, he wouldn't withdraw his love or dissolve his covenants: "I the Lord do not change. So you, O descendants of Jacob, are not destroyed" (3:6). God said, "Return to me, and I will return to you" (3:7).

Apparently, some people who heard Malachi's messages repented of their sin (3:16). God graciously encouraged them: "But for you who revere my name the sun of righteousness will rise with healing in its rays. And you will go out and frolic like well-fed calves" (4:2).

Like Malachi's listeners, we struggle to love God as we should. We too dishonor his name and ignore our relationship with him. We respond to his grace with second-rate gifts and hollow worship. He sends us a similar message: I love you so much that I sent Jesus to earth. If you repent of your sins and accept him as your savior, you will be healed. He will fill you with so much joy that you'll skip around like satisfied calves in a sun-drenched field of grain.

We won't receive a Christmas card from God in our mailbox this year. His Christmas message to us is contained in his Word—both the written word and the Living Word, Jesus Christ. What will be our response to his message?

DIG DEEPER

1. In Malachi chapter one, God asks a series of questions in verses 6, 8, 9, and 13. How would you respond if he asked you those questions?

2. Malachi, whose name means "my messenger," speaks of another messenger God was going to send to his people (3:1). Who was it? Read Matthew 11:7–15.

3. In Matthew 28:18–20 Jesus commissions the disciples (and us) as his messengers. What are the characteristics of a good messenger? Read Malachi 2:5–7.

4. The last two words of the Old Testament are "total destruction" (Malachi 4:6). Adam and Eve's disobedience brought sin's destruction into the world (Genesis 3:14–19). Jesus removed it (Galatians 3:13–14). When will the effects of sin be eradicated? Read Romans 8:18–25 and Revelation 22:3.

December 15: The Forever Promises

Mary said, *"He has helped his servant Israel, remembering to be merciful to Abraham and his descendants forever, just as he promised our ancestors."* Luke 1:54–55

Forever. Do you know anything that lasts forever? Mary's prayer in Luke 1 spoke of God's faithfulness in remembering his promises to bless Abraham's descendants forever. God also promised that the whole world would be blessed through Abraham's descendants and that kings would descend from him (Genesis 17:6).

The angel Gabriel told Mary that her son Jesus would be given "the throne of his father David, and he [would] reign over Jacob's descendants forever; his kingdom will never end" (Luke 1:32–33). Mary probably remembered a promise God gave to one of Abraham's descendants, King David: "If your sons keep my covenant and the statutes I teach them, then their sons will sit on your throne for ever and ever" (Psalm 132:12).

Had Israel expected David's son Solomon to be the forever king? He was the wisest man who ever lived, and he built the magnificent temple. However, God's promise to David had been conditional. Solomon disobeyed God, ignoring his warning that amassing material things would lead to pride and cause him to forget the Lord (Deuteronomy 8:11–14). After Solomon's forty-year reign, the kingdom split, and eventually David's throne was empty.

But God is faithful to his promises even when we aren't faithful. One of the prophets wrote, "A shoot will come up from the stump of Jesse; from his roots a Branch will bear

65

fruit" (Isaiah 11:1). Only a stump remained, but David's lineage lasted until the birth of Jesus.

Unlike Solomon, Jesus lived a sinless life. He kept God's covenant and laws perfectly. Jesus said, "My kingdom is not of this world ... my kingdom is from another place" (John 18:36). For now, Jesus's reign on earth isn't fully what it will be. But one day he'll return to reign in absolute power. An announcement will ring out from heaven: "The kingdom of the world has become the kingdom of our Lord and of his Messiah, and he will reign for ever and ever" (Revelation 11:15).

Jesus taught his disciples (including us) to pray, "your kingdom come, your will be done, on earth as it is in heaven" (Matthew 6:10). As you pray, ponder God's faithfulness in keeping his promises forever.

DIG DEEPER

1. Another Scripture passage Mary may be thinking of in Luke 1 is Psalm 145:10–13. How is the kingdom described in those verses?

2. According to Romans 4:13–25, who are the promised descendants of Abraham?

3. Read Luke 1:5–25, 57–80. Why do you think God gave a miracle baby to Zechariah and Elizabeth in their old age? How did it encourage the people of Israel who hadn't seen a miracle or heard a prophecy in 400 years?

December 16: The Family Tree

The Lord said to Abraham, *"I will surely bless you and make your descendants as numerous as the stars in the sky and as the sand on the seashore. Your descendants will take possession of the cities of their enemies, and through your offspring all nations on earth will be blessed, because you have obeyed me."* Genesis 22:17–18

What kind of people would you expect to find in Jesus Christ's genealogy? Saintly paragons of virtue? There aren't any of those. In fact, some were people you'd want to hide—those proverbial "skeletons in your closet"! Our merciful God used ordinary flawed people (like us) to bring about the extraordinary birth of his Son.

Genealogies may seem boring—all those names, many unpronounceable. But Matthew's genealogy of Jesus is definitely not boring when you study it (Matthew 1:1–17). On close examination, you'll see that it's not a typical family tree with branches from both sides of the family and twigs that represent all the siblings. This genealogy is a straight line from Abraham to Jesus, from father (and sometimes mother) to one child to one child, and so on.

Unlike most ancient Jewish genealogies, Matthew includes the names of five women: Tamar, Rahab, Ruth, Bathsheba (Uriah's wife), and Mary. And the line of descent doesn't always run through the oldest son.

Matthew's genealogy begins with a miraculous birth. Abraham, who was a hundred years old, and Sarah, who was ninety, produced a child. Impossible! But they received a promise, "Is anything too hard for the Lord? I will return to you at the appointed time next year and Sarah will have a son" (Genesis 18:14). Isaac was born nine months later just as God had promised.

Abraham only had one child with Sarah; Isaac was the child of God's promise, the heir that began the Messiah's line of descent from Abraham.

At the end of Matthew's genealogy, by an even greater miracle, a virgin named Mary conceived a child by the Holy Spirit and gave birth to Jesus (1:18–25).

But God's family tree doesn't end there. By another miraculous birth—a spiritual birth—believers become children of Abraham, God's children (Galatians 3:6–7). That fulfills the promise to Abraham that all nations on earth will be blessed through his offspring, that is, through Jesus Christ.

This year don't skip over the genealogies in the Christmas story. Read them and rejoice! Then celebrate your placement in God's family tree.

DIG DEEPER

1. Read Romans 9:1–8. What does Paul say about the children of the promise, God's children?

2. Does it surprise you to find ordinary, flawed people in the genealogy of Jesus? Why should that please you? Read 1 Corinthians 1:26–31.

3. Luke also gives a genealogy of Jesus. Read Luke 3:23–38. How is his different from Matthew's? What do you think Luke is trying to emphasize?

December 17: The Need for a Savior

There is no one righteous, not even one; there is no one who understands; there is no one who seeks God. Romans 3:10–11

It's a sordid story. But many stories of mercy and grace are. Judah was the fourth of Jacob's twelve sons. In Genesis 38, he committed a series of sins. First, he married a Canaanite woman. Years later, he assured his widowed daughter-in-law, Tamar, that she could marry his youngest son, then refused to honor the promise. After Judah's wife died, he had sexual relations with a woman he thought was a prostitute.

The woman was Tamar, disguised as a prostitute and determined to bear a son who could claim her dead husband's inheritance. Although Scriptures such as Genesis 38:8–10 and Deuteronomy 25:5–10 indicate that her motives were justifiable, Tamar's methods were not. She harbored resentment against her father-in-law Judah, deceived him, and had sexual relations with him.

Yet God allowed Tamar to conceive and bear twin sons: Perez and Zerah. And even though Judah's other son, Shelah, was older than Perez, God selected Perez as an ancestor of Jesus Christ. Why would he do that?

The foolish, flawed ancestors of Jesus illustrate how unconditionally God loves his people, how determined he is to redeem them, and how completely he forgives them when they repent.

Although the Bible doesn't mention Tamar again in Genesis, we do know more about Judah. He was the brother who finally took responsibility for the crimes he and his siblings had committed against Joseph. First, he claimed full responsibility for Benjamin's safety in Genesis 43:8–9; he then offered his own life in exchange for Benjamin's in Genesis 44:33.

God rewarded Judah for these sacrificial acts by choosing him as the progenitor of both the royal and messianic line (Genesis 49:8–12). Tamar is also honored because the line of descent passed through her son, and she is mentioned by name in the gospel of Matthew's genealogy.

Oh how merciful our God is! We're all Judahs and Tamars. Ensnared by error. Shackled by sin. Deserving punishment, but offered forgiveness. Thanks be to God for providing the solution: a Savior, who is Christ the Lord.

Are you rejoicing in the glorious truth of redemption this Christmas?

DIG DEEPER

1. What similarities and differences do you see between the Judah of Genesis 38:8–10 and the Judah of Genesis 43:8–9 and 44:33? What do you think prompted his later actions?

2. Reflect on your own need for a Savior by reading Romans 3:9–20. Then celebrate the gift of God's Son by reading Romans 3:21–24.

3. Is there a loved one in your life who's resisting God's gift of salvation? Read Jeremiah 31:3 and 2 Peter 3:8–9. Don't despair. Keep praying.

4. David used the Hebrew word for *savior*, *yasha*, in 2 Samuel 22:3.[9] David wrote this hymn (recorded in both 2 Samuel 22 and Psalm 18) as a tribute to his mighty Savior who had delivered him from so many troubles. After you read David's hymn, take time to praise your Savior for all the times he has delivered you.

December 18: A Scarlet Cord

By faith the walls of Jericho fell, after the army had marched around them for seven days. By faith the prostitute Rahab, because she welcomed the spies, was not killed with those who were disobedient. Hebrews 11:30–31

The battle of Jericho was unusual (Joshua 6:1–25). Joshua and the army marched around the city once a day for six days and then on the seventh day marched around it seven times. For six days, the people marched silently while seven priests sounded ram horns. But after a long blast from the ram horns on the seventh day, they gave a great shout. "And the walls came tumbling down" as many of us sang as children.

When the walls of the city tumbled, only one small section of wall remained standing: the house where a prostitute named Rahab and her family had gathered. These people were the only ones spared—in spite of the fact that they were Canaanites, in spite of Rahab's sinful past.

Rahab believed in the God of the Israelites. She had heard about how he'd helped his people fight their enemies. And when Jericho was next, Rahab hid the two spies Joshua sent so the men of the city wouldn't kill them. In return, she asked that her family be spared. The spies told her to hang from her window the scarlet cord by which she'd let down the two escapees (Joshua 2:1–25).

Rahab trusted God and believed he would allow her family to escape the coming destruction of the city. She was a prostitute, a Gentile, and yet she's listed in Christ's ancestry (Matthew 1:5).

God didn't condemn Rahab for her past sins. He saw her heart of faith. He saw her willingness to leave her old life behind and go wherever God took her. She had no idea she'd be an ancestor of the Messiah.

Rahab's scarlet cord looked forward symbolically to Jesus's sacrificial death, his shed blood, his taking the judgment for sinners upon himself on the cross.

Do you feel condemned by past sins this Christmas? Don't believe the lie. You are not condemned; those sins were nailed to the cross. God sees your heart of faith. Leave your old life behind and follow him wherever he takes you. You never know how he will use your life.

DIG DEEPER

1. Read Luke 7:36–48. How did Jesus respond to this woman who had "lived a sinful life"?

2. God's grace and salvation are offered to all, including women like Rahab. But according to Colossians 3:1–14, what should we put off and put on in order to freely enjoy our new lives in Christ? What specifically do you need to put off from your past, and with what will you replace it?

3. Compare Rahab's scarlet cord (Joshua 6:1–25) and the blood put on doorposts (Exodus 12:7–23). How was each a sign of faith?

4. You don't need to hang a scarlet cord outside your window. How can you know you are sealed and protected from God's judgment? See 2 Corinthians 1:21–22.

Restore the Joy: Daily Devotions for December

80

December 19: A Kinsman-Redeemer

For your Maker is your husband—the Lord Almighty is his name—the Holy One of Israel is your Redeemer; he is called the God of all the earth. Isaiah 54:5

If the mothers in tenth-century-BC Bethlehem had passed around a "Most Eligible Bachelors" list at the town well, Boaz's name would've been on it.

Everything the Bible says about Boaz is admirable. He was devout. He acknowledged the Lord's sovereignty over both his business and personal affairs; he obeyed the levitical laws about gleaning (Leviticus 19:9–10). He was a gentleman. He treated his workers and gleaners with the same gracious, respectful attitude that he used at the city gate when he addressed the elders. He was discerning. When Ruth, an impoverished widow, gleaned in Boaz's fields, he recognized her stellar character and rewarded it. He then protected her from both the advances of less noble men and town gossip.

When Ruth told her mother-in-law, Naomi, about Boaz's kindness and generosity, Naomi was pleased. She remembered that Boaz was one of her husband's relatives and could act as a *ga'al*, a kinsman-redeemer.[10]

The role of the *ga'al* is described in Leviticus 25:24–25. If a paternal estate had been sold, the nearest living male relative could buy back the property so it would remain in the family. Boaz chose not only to redeem the property but also to marry the widow, Ruth, so her first husband's branch of the family would have an heir.

Ruth came to Bethlehem as a helpless widow, without a livelihood or a future. But she found grace in the eyes of Boaz and became a chief resident of the city, secure in the love and the prosperity of her new husband. God rewarded Boaz and Ruth with a son, Obed, who was the grandfather of Israel's greatest earthly king, David, and an ancestor of the King of Kings, Jesus Christ.

God has provided each of us with a Boaz. Jesus Christ has plucked us from the fields of spiritual poverty, shame, and hopelessness. He has made us his bride and given us his name. We will live forever under his protection and enjoy forever his abundance.

Glory to God in the highest! Our kinsman-redeemer has come. What blessings are you enjoying today because of your kinsman-redeemer?

DIG DEEPER

1. Read Ruth 1–4 this week. As you read, make a list of all the ways in which Boaz is symbolic of Jesus Christ. Then thank Jesus for being your kinsman-redeemer.

2. Both Ruth (a Moabite) and Rahab (a Canaanite) were Gentiles. They were grafted into Abraham's family tree. Why is that significant? Read Romans 4:1–12 and 11:13–22.

3. Christ is not only our redeemer, but he's also our husband. What privileges does that give us? See Ephesians 2:4–7, Revelation 5:10, and Revelation 19:7–9.

December 20: Eternal Three-in-One

Gabriel told Mary, *"The Holy Spirit will come on you, and the power of the Most High will overshadow you."* (Luke 1:35)

James Montgomery was a Scotsman who invested most of his adult life in the publication of a newspaper in Sheffield, England. However, his avocation was poetry and hymn writing—he wrote at least eleven books and over 400 hymns.[11]

"Angels from the Realms of Glory" is perhaps the most well known hymn Montgomery wrote. In it, he created a remarkable tapestry of the whole story of redemption, paying tribute to creation in the first stanza, the crucifixion in the fifth stanza, and the eternal reign of Christ in the last two stanzas.

The final stanza is particularly intriguing because Montgomery had the foresight to include all three persons of the Trinity:

> All creation, join in praising
> God, the Father, Spirit, Son,
> Evermore your voices raising
> To th'eternal Three in One.

Not many Christmas carols do that. But acknowledging that all three persons of the Godhead were involved in Christ's mission on earth should be part of our Christmas worship.

Gabriel told Mary that "the power of the Most High" would overshadow her. Old Testament writers referred to God Most High (*El Elyon*) when they wanted to emphasize

God's sovereignty over all people, both Jew and Gentile. It's a name Mary and her contemporaries would have associated with Jehovah, God the Father.

The angel who came to Joseph said, "What is conceived of her is from the Holy Spirit" (Matthew 1:20). And then the angel refers to Isaiah's prophecy: the birth of Jesus meant that God (*theos*) had descended to earth (vv. 22–23). *Theos* is the Greek word used throughout the New Testament to represent all three persons of the Godhead. When New Testament writers wanted to indicate a specific member of the Trinity they used phrases like "Spirit of God," "Son of God," and "God the Father."

This Christmas season as you sing the familiar advent songs, look for references to God the Father and to the Holy Spirit. Whisper a prayer of thanks to each person of the Trinity for his role in the redemption story that began in Genesis and ends in Revelation.

DIG DEEPER

1. Read Luke 1:26–45. What was the role of the Holy Spirit in these events?

2. The name God Most High is first mentioned in Genesis 14:18 when Abraham met Melchizedek, a Gentile priest. To gain a clearer picture of what this name signifies in the Old Testament, read Psalm 47 and Psalm 83.

3. *Immanuel* means "God *(theos)* is with us." How were all three persons of the Godhead present when Jesus was on earth? Luke 2:25–38 and Matthew 3:3–17 give two examples.

·

"Angels from the Realms of Glory"

James Montgomery, 1816
Public Domain

Angels from the realms of glory,
Wing your flight o'er all the earth;
Ye who sang creation's story
Now proclaim Messiah's birth.

Refrain:
Come and worship, come and worship,
Worship Christ, the newborn King.

Shepherds, in the field abiding,
Watching o'er your flocks by night,
God with us is now residing;
Yonder shines the infant light:

Sages, leave your contemplations,
Brighter visions beam afar;
Seek the great Desire of nations;
Ye have seen His natal star.

Saints, before the altar bending,
Watching long in hope and fear;
Suddenly the Lord, descending,
In His temple shall appear.

Sinners, wrung with true repentance,
Doomed for guilt to endless pains,
Justice now revokes the sentence,
Mercy calls you; break your chains.

Though an Infant now we view Him,
He shall fill His Father's throne,
Gather all the nations to Him;
Every knee shall then bow down:

All creation, join in praising
God, the Father, Spirit, Son,
Evermore your voices raising
To th'eternal Three in One.

December 21: Mary's Mind-set

And Mary said: "My soul magnifies the Lord." Luke 1:46 (NKJV)

Magnify. The Greek word is *megalyno*: "to make great, to make conspicuous; to esteem highly, to extol, laud, and celebrate."[12] It brings to mind an image of a servant bowing low before a monarch.

Maybe that's one reason Mary used *magnify* in her prayer. God's messenger Gabriel had given Mary's son two royal titles: He was the son of *El Elyon*, the Most High God who reigns over the universe; he was also the son of David and would reign over the house of Jacob (Luke 1:32–33). Mary, however, humbled herself before the One who bestowed the honor instead of celebrating her improved standing as the mother of a king.

Mary also may have been referencing one of King David's psalms in her prayer: "Oh, magnify the Lord with me, and let us exalt his name together" (Psalm 34:3 NKJV). If so, the psalm has other connections to Mary's situation and her mind-set.

In Psalm 34:4, David said that God had delivered him from all his fears. Luke 1:29 says Mary was "greatly troubled" when Gabriel appeared. He sensed her fear and said, "Do not be afraid" (v. 30). Perhaps God delivered Mary from fear before she told her parents and Joseph about Gabriel's visit. She expressed no fear in this prayer.

Second, Psalm 34:5–6 says, "those who look to him are radiant; their faces are never covered with shame." What rumors spread throughout Nazareth after Mary returned from her three-month visit to Elizabeth (Luke 1:56)? What did friends and relatives think when they saw a visibly pregnant Mary? Gabriel said the Holy Spirit had come upon Mary (1:35). But how many people believed that—before or after Jesus's birth?

Mary may have battled fear and shame, but her prayer affirms her unshakeable trust in God. She chose to magnify him and to celebrate his goodness regardless of what circumstances indicated or people said.

Has fear or shame stolen your joy this Christmas? Maybe you've lost a loved one or a job has been ripped from your grasp. Maybe you simply dread spending another holiday season alone. Choose Mary's mind-set. Trust God's plan for you. Wait confidently for his wisdom and deliverance. He loves you and his hand of blessing rests on your shoulder. Choose to magnify the Lord.

DIG DEEPER

1. Read Psalm 34:1–22. Look for other ways that the promises of this psalm could have encouraged Mary during her pregnancy. Which of its promises encourages you?

2. Paul uses *megalyno* in Philippians 1:20—"that now as always Christ will be exalted in my body." What can you do this Christmas to exalt Christ in your home or community?

3. Mary's prayer is similar to Hannah's prayer in 1 Samuel 2:1–10. What truths about God and his relationship with people are emphasized in both prayers?

4. Read Psalm 138. Which of its truths would have comforted Mary? With whom can you share this psalm's message of hope and assurance?

December 22: The Joy of Salvation

Mary said, *"And my spirit has rejoiced in God my Savior."* Luke 1:47

The angel Gabriel ended his announcement to Mary with news about a relative named Elizabeth. Although formerly unable to conceive, this woman was now six months pregnant in spite of the fact that she was very old (Luke 1:36).

After Gabriel left, Mary "got ready and hurried" to visit Elizabeth (vv. 39–40). Both women were filled with joy at the news the angel had brought. Moreover, the baby in Elizabeth's womb leaped for joy at Mary's greeting (v. 41). Elizabeth's baby was John the Baptist who prepared the way for Jesus before either baby was born.

Mary's words in Luke 1:47 echoed David's in Psalm 35:9, "And my soul shall be joyful in the Lord; it shall rejoice in his salvation" (NKJV).

Joy is not the same as happiness. The joy Mary, Elizabeth, John the Baptist, and David experienced didn't depend on circumstances. Joy is "an inner sense of exultation and confidence in God, which the Holy Spirit works in the lives of believers and which we experience despite present sufferings"[13]

Jesus, with his death and resurrection, saved us from our sins. But he has not yet saved us from our enemies. Like David, we'll have battles with enemies all our lives. But we can say as he did, "You prepare a table before me in the presence of my enemies. You anoint my head with oil; my cup overflows" (Psalm 23:5). Our cups overflow with inner joy because we have a salvation that can never be touched by our enemies. One day we'll see all our enemies forever defeated, including our biggest enemy: death (1 Corinthians 15:24–26).

Mary and the rest of the Jewish nation had long awaited a Messiah who would save his people. And now he had come. Since Jesus Christ's first coming—his death, resurrection, and ascension—we have waited a long time. Can you imagine the joy we'll experience at his second coming when he achieves total victory?

Have you noticed how often the word *joy* is used in the carols you hear and sing during the Christmas season? How many of those songs—including "Joy to the World"—speak of both Jesus's first and second coming?

DIG DEEPER

1. In Exodus 15:1–3 what does Moses say about joy and salvation? According to Exodus 14, what was the occasion and what part had Moses and the people played in the victory?

2. In 1 Peter 1:3–13, what reasons does he give for our "inexpressible and glorious joy"?

3. According to Jude 1:24–25, what is Jesus doing for us right now, and what will he do when we stand before God the Father?

December 23: God's Mighty Arm

Mary said, *"He has performed mighty deeds with his arm; he has scattered those who are proud in their inmost thoughts."* Luke 1:51

The skinny little kid, beaten by bigger kids, limped home, then returned with his father. The six-foot-four man wore a sleeveless shirt, baring his bulging muscles. Although he didn't say a word, the belittled bullies ran away screaming.

Mary remembered many instances where God showed his mighty arm and scattered his enemies. She knew God's Word—what we call the Old Testament. Perhaps she thought of the exodus when God delivered his people from their Egyptian oppressors. Maybe she thought of David's psalms where he sang of God's victories over his enemies: "for he has done marvelous things; his right hand and his holy arm have worked salvation for him" (Psalm 98:1).

The expression "arm of God" is anthropomorphic; that is, it describes God as having human form or attributes. But God doesn't have a physical body—he is spirit. In Scripture, his arm is symbolic of the strength and power he displays on earth when he delivers from bondage, saves from sin, and judges his enemies.

Mary knew that those who had reason to be proud of their accomplishments, those with arrogant "inmost thoughts" but no knowledge of God and his revelation of himself, would be scattered—they'd vanish.

Mary also may have been thinking of another psalm: "Shouts of joy and victory resound in the tents of the righteous: 'The Lord's right hand has done mighty things!'" (Psalm 118:15). Soon joyous shouts of victory would resound—not from great palaces but from a humble place where a young couple who had few earthly possessions gazed in wonder at a miraculous baby.

The prophets had said that one day a virgin would conceive and bear a son (Isaiah 7:14). Mary's child would one day display his mighty arm in miracles and victory over death. He would resurrect from the dead. Now he sits at the right hand (arm) of God, near his Father's ear, and intercedes for the people of God (Hebrews 7:23–25).

Like Mary, can you sing of mighty deeds God has performed with power and deliverance in your life?

DIG DEEPER

1. Read Psalm 98:1–9. Many songs in the book of Psalms celebrate what God had done in the past, especially in helping Israel. Can you rewrite the lyrics of this song, explaining what God sent his Son to do on earth?

2. Besides strength and power, what picture does Isaiah 40:9–11 give of the work of God's arm?

3. To what does Jesus attribute his ability to cast out demons in Luke 11:14–22?

4. What is the answer to Isaiah's question in 53:1, that is, to whom is the arm of God revealed according to John 12:37–43? What must a person have in order to see the mighty power of God?

December 24: God with Us

All this took place to fulfill what the Lord had said through the prophet: "The virgin will be with child and will give birth to a son, and they will call him Immanuel (which means, 'God with us')." Matthew 1:22–23

One rainy night my husband, Ken, went to a colleague's retirement dinner. An hour and a half after I thought he'd be home, I began to worry. I tried praying, but mostly I stared out the window or paced the floor.

Ken was driving my car because his car was being repaired following a minor accident. I felt guilty because I'd forgotten to tell him that my car needed gas. I worried that he'd run out of gas and that an inattentive driver, unable to stop on the wet pavement, might ram the car from behind.

"I am with you," God whispered as I paced. "I'm also with Ken."

I remembered the Scripture passage in Isaiah I had read earlier in the day as I researched the word *Immanuel*. I had judged Ahaz for turning to the Assyrians for help instead of trusting God. How could Ahaz turn to the cruelest nation? The Assyrians would eventually become Israel's enemy. Isaiah offered to ask God for a sign that he was with his people, but Ahaz would not ask for a sign. Isaiah said, "Therefore the Lord himself shall give you a sign; behold, a virgin shall conceive, and bear a son, and shall call his name Immanuel" (Isaiah 7:1–14). God was with his people.

That evening when I worried, "Where could my husband be? What could have happened?" I had turned to a cruel enemy, Satan. He gladly presented all kinds of dreadful scenarios and guilty feelings. Instead, I should have trusted that God was with me and with Ken.

In repentance, I asked God for his peace and received it. God is with us. And he is with our loved ones when they drive slowly through the rain, stop for gas, and arrive home safely.

What are you fearful or worried about? Ask God to give you peace and the assurance of his presence.

DIG DEEPER

1. Read Ahaz's story in Isaiah 7 and 8 (especially 7:3 and 8:3). The message about Immanuel is a prophecy within a prophecy. What messages did God give his people in Ahaz's time through the birth of Isaiah's children and their names?

2. Read Philippians 4:6–9. What does it mean that God is with us? Should that make a difference in how we live? What happens when we go to God with our fears?

3. Read Psalm 139:1–16. According to the psalmist, in what specific places is God with us?

December 25: An Ordinary Couple

For we do not have a high priest who is unable to sympathize with our weaknesses, but we have one who has been tempted in every way, just as we are—yet did not sin. Hebrews 4:15

Can you imagine Mary as she looked eagerly at the tiny bundle of flesh that Joseph held in his hands? As he placed the baby in her arms and sat beside her to look at him, what could Joseph have been thinking? What did they expect to see?

The baby didn't glow. His head wasn't circled by a halo. He looked like other newborns they'd seen. He had ten tiny fingers, ten tiny toes. His red wrinkly face protested the travail he'd just experienced.

Often we see idealized manger scenes, some of them fancy crystal crèches, and we forget how ordinary this event looked in spite of the identity of this extraordinary baby.

Joseph and Mary knew the miraculous circumstances behind the conception: she was a virgin and had conceived by the Holy Spirit. Before Jesus began kicking at Mary from the womb—gentle nudges to acknowledge his presence and eagerness to be born—Joseph and Mary had each been visited by angels. They hadn't spent hours choosing a name: the angel told each of them that the baby's name would be Jesus, derived from the Hebrew word *Yeshua,* which meant "savior" or "Jehovah saves" (Matthew 1:18–25).[14]

The people of Israel had long anticipated a savior, a Messiah, because God had made promises to Abraham, King David, and through the prophets. Now Joseph and Mary looked into the face of someone like them and yet not like them at all.

As you look at the tiny babe in the manger this Christmas, can you feel the awe Joseph and Mary must have felt as God broke into history to dwell with his people and become their Savior?

DIG DEEPER

1. Read Luke 1:26–38. What else did the angel tell Mary besides the name she was to give her child?

2. What promise was repeated in these Old Testament prophecies: Isaiah 40:2; 53:6; Jeremiah 31:31–34; Ezekiel 36:25–27; Daniel 9:24; Zechariah 13:1?

3. Read Exodus 19:12–25 and Hebrews 12:18–24. Why do you think the coming of God to meet his people at Mt. Sinai was so different from the coming of Jesus at Bethlehem?

December 26: What Do You Expect?

When John, who was in prison, heard about the deeds of the Messiah, he sent his disciples to ask him, "Are you the one who is to come, or should we expect someone else?"
Matthew 11:2–3

Did Christmas disappoint you? Did your loved ones neglect to give you the present you wanted? Did squabbling siblings get you down? Did snow interfere with your holiday celebrations?

Jesus's earthly ministry disappointed many people. He came to set the captives free, and yet John the Baptist wasn't just imprisoned, he was beheaded (Matthew 14:10). The Pharisees expected the Messiah to honor them and to fulfill the Law as they understood it. But Jesus condemned the Pharisee's hypocrisy, their greed, and their misinterpretation of the Law (Matthew 23:13–29).

The people escorted Jesus into Jerusalem with the equivalent of a ticker-tape parade because they expected him to save them from their oppressors and reign as David's heir. They didn't realize that he came as the Servant of the Lord to die for the sins of his people. He rode a donkey, a sign that he came in peace, rather than a war-horse, which a conqueror would have ridden.

Jesus's disciples were disappointed when he didn't show any political ambition. Although he told them several times that he was going to Jerusalem to die, the disciples didn't understand what he meant. Even on the night before his death, the disciples disputed which of them was considered to be greatest, confident that Jesus was about to become king (Luke 22:24).

Sometimes we're disappointed with Jesus. He doesn't seem to be the Savior we expected. Our problem is that we don't see the whole picture. The Bible reveals two comings of Jesus, the Messiah. We live between those two advents. Jesus fulfilled many of the Old Testament promises in his first coming, but many more will be fulfilled when he comes again.

He will not come as a humble servant the next time. He will come as King of Kings riding on a white horse as conqueror making war on his enemies, including sin and death (Revelation 19:11 and 21:4). We will not be disappointed!

Charles Wesley's hymn, "Come, Thou Long-Expected Jesus," anticipates this second coming:

> Come, Thou long-expected Jesus,
> Born to set Thy people free
> From our fears and sin release us,
> Let us find our rest in Thee.

Wesley's second verse includes the line, "Now Thy gracious kingdom bring." May that be our prayer too as we wait for Jesus to return.

DIG DEEPER

1. Read Psalm 110:1. Where is Jesus right now? When will he return?

2. Read Revelation 19:11–21 and Revelation 21:1–7. What does Jesus promise to do when he returns? Do his promises alarm you or encourage you? Why?

3. Wesley wrote "Let us find our rest in Thee." How can we do that? Read Psalm 37:7 and Matthew 11:28–29.

"Come, Thou Long Expected Jesus"

Charles Wesley, 1745
Public Domain

Come, Thou long expected Jesus
Born to set Thy people free;
From our fears and sins release us,
Let us find our rest in Thee.
Israel's Strength and Consolation,
Hope of all the earth Thou art;
Dear Desire of every nation,
Joy of every longing heart.

Born Thy people to deliver,
Born a child and yet a King,
Born to reign in us forever,
Now Thy gracious kingdom bring.
By Thine own eternal Spirit
Rule in all our hearts alone;
By Thine all sufficient merit,
Raise us to Thy glorious throne.

December 27: Two Senior Citizens

Simeon said, *"Lord, now you are letting your servant depart in peace, according to your word; for my eyes have seen your salvation."* Luke 2:29–30 (ESV)

The Christmas message is one of hope for all. Jesus came as a helpless baby to a poor couple. His birth wasn't announced to great leaders but to outcast shepherds and two senior citizens.

We aren't told how old Simeon was or even who he was—possibly a priest. We do know that he was a faithful man who knew the Scriptures. Simeon was focused. He had one purpose to fulfill before he died. The Holy Spirit had revealed to him that he would not see death before he had seen the Christ, the Messiah (Luke 2:26).

One day, led by the Spirit into the temple, he saw a young couple who had come to dedicate their baby. This happened almost every day, for the Law required every firstborn forty-day-old male child to be dedicated (Exodus 13:2,12; Leviticus 12:6). When Simeon took the child into his arms, the Holy Spirit told him that this was the One for whom he had been waiting—this baby was the Christ.

As Simeon prayed for the child, the Spirit gave him prophetic words:

- "In the sight of all nations"—Simeon spoke in the Outer Court of the temple where even women and non-Israelites were allowed (Luke 2:31).

- "A light for revelation to the Gentiles"—God was revealing something that extended far beyond the Israelites (Luke 2:32).
- "The glory of your people Israel"—but through this, Israel would be glorified (Luke 2:32).

Simeon had barely finished speaking when Anna, a prophetess, came up and confirmed his message. Anna, an eighty-four-year-old widow, "never left the temple but worshiped night and day, fasting and praying" (Luke 2:37). Full of excitement, she gave thanks to God and hurried off to tell others she knew were also waiting for "the redemption of Jerusalem" (v. 38). These two seniors were the first to publicly announce the coming of the Christ.

We may lose physical strength and abilities as we grow older, but through the Holy Spirit, God gives us inner strength and gifts to use to benefit others.

How can you use the gifts God gave you to serve others?

DIG DEEPER

1. How does Luke 2:25–38 describe the faith of Anna and Simeon?

2. Read Psalm 39:4–5. How does the psalmist describe life? What does it mean to number our days? (See also Psalm 90:12.)

3. Read 1 Corinthians 12:1–28. What are the gifts God has given you that could benefit others?

December 28: Renewed Resolve

David said, *"And you, my son Solomon, acknowledge the God of your father and serve him with wholehearted devotion and with a willing mind, for the Lord searches every heart and understands every desire and every thought."* 1 Chronicles 28:9

It was both the end and the beginning.

King David stood before the thousands who had gathered, and he delivered what may have been his last public address. His heir, Solomon, was "young and inexperienced." Solomon's task was monumental because the palatial structure he would build was "not for man but for the Lord God" (1 Chronicles 29:1–2).

God had given David the blueprint; then David had amassed the materials. But Solomon would organize the laborers as well as supervise the construction and completion of the work. However, before one stone was laid, something else had to be settled. David asked, "Who is willing to consecrate themselves to the Lord today?" (v. 5)

To consecrate is to set aside for God's service. In this case, David asked the people to give generous offerings, as he had done, so the temple could be completed. And David rejoiced when the people gave materials for the temple "freely and wholeheartedly" (v. 9).

But that was not enough. David also understood that no task, great or small, could be accomplished without wholehearted devotion and pure-hearted motivation. Notice what he says in his prayer: "Lord, the God of our fathers Abraham, Isaac and Israel, keep these desires and thoughts in the hearts of your people forever, and keep their hearts loyal to you" (v 18). What desire? The desire to give both their possessions and their devotion "willingly and with honest intent" (v. 17).

In spiritual matters, we're all young and inexperienced— unable to carry out God's will without divine guidance. The task before us is great also—our bodies must be dwelling places fit for a holy God (1 Corinthians 6:19-20). And we are also laborers in God's greater work—the building of his church. We too must consecrate ourselves for his service— set aside everything that detracts from our ability to serve him with wholehearted devotion.

The end of a year provides an opportunity to evaluate the quality of our spiritual endeavors. Let us begin this new year with a renewed resolve to keep our hearts loyal to our king and to serve him "willingly and with honest intent."

DIG DEEPER

1. Study the organization of David's prayer in 1 Chronicles 29:10–19. What comes first? What comes last? What can we learn from the way he prayed?

2. Compare David's words in 1 Chronicles 29:15–18 with Paul's words in 2 Corinthians 8:8–12. In what ways are their attitudes about giving similar?

3. Four times in his prayer, David affirms that all we have comes from God. Why is it so important to remember that? Read Psalm 49.

December 29: Sunless Days

There will be no more night. They will not need the light of a lamp or the light of the sun, for the Lord God will give them light. And they will reign for ever and ever. Revelation 22:5

The lights appear at one house, then another, and another. Certain houses or neighborhoods are so spectacularly lit that people go out of their way to see the displays. I love these lights because they illuminate the darkest nights of the year when the sun shines less and less each day.

Many Christmas songs celebrate the star that lit up the night sky and led magi thousands of miles to Bethlehem. In the Christmas hymn "As with Gladness Men of Old," hymn writer William C. Dix (born 1837) likened the magi's journey led by the star's light to the Christian life.

As we consider the magi who followed the light, the hymn encourages us to pray: "so, most Gracious Lord, may we evermore your splendor see." As they knelt in adoration, "so may we with willing feet ever seek your mercy seat." As they offered rare gifts, may we "all our costliest treasures bring, Christ, to you, our heavenly King."

The last two stanzas of Dix's hymn ask the "Holy Jesus" to keep us in the narrow way as long as we live:

> And when mortal things are past,
> Bring our ransomed lives at last
> Where they need no star to guide,
> Where no clouds your glory hide.

125

Then the hymn celebrates the brightest lights ever displayed:

> In that glorious city bright
> None shall need created light;
> You its light, its joy, its crown,
> You its sun which goes not down;
> There forever may we sing
> Alleluias to our King!

We don't have to wait until we die and go to heaven to walk in light. Jesus said, "I am the light of the world. Whoever follows me will never walk in darkness, but will have the light of life" (John 8:12). Although we still need the sun to light our earthly days, we have the "light of life" shining inside us no matter how dark our circumstances.

The Christmas light displays soon will be taken down and stored until next year, but the Light of the World shines in ours heart every day. We can celebrate his light even on sunless days.

DIG DEEPER

1. It's easy to think of the magi as characters in a story or Christmas play, but they were real. Read their story in Matthew 2:1–12. Compare their search for Jesus with yours. How did they respond and how did you respond?

2. The magi might have known Old Testament prophecies because Jews had been in Babylon during the years of their captivity. Israelites understood that Balaam's prophecy in Numbers 24:17 pointed to a messiah, a deliverer. What did Balaam's prophecy tell the magi?

3. Using a concordance or another source such as blueletterbible.org, do a word study on the word *light*. You can start your search with these verses: Matthew 5:14–16 and 1 John 1:5–7. How can you improve your walk in the light?

"As with Gladness Men of Old"

William C. Dix, 1860
Public Domain

As with gladness, men of old
Did the guiding star behold
As with joy they hailed its light
Leading onward, beaming bright
So, most glorious Lord, may we
Evermore be led to Thee.

As with joyful steps they sped
To that lowly manger bed
There to bend the knee before
Him Whom Heaven and earth adore;
So may we with willing feet
Ever seek Thy mercy seat.

As they offered gifts most rare
At that manger rude and bare;
So may we with holy joy,
Pure and free from sin's alloy,
All our costliest treasures bring,
Christ, to Thee, our heavenly King.

Holy Jesus, every day
Keep us in the narrow way;
And, when earthly things are past,
Bring our ransomed souls at last
Where they need no star to guide,
Where no clouds Thy glory hide.

In the heavenly country bright,
Need they no created light;
Thou its Light, its Joy, its Crown,
Thou its Sun which goes not down;
There forever may we sing
Alleluias to our King!

December 30: By Another Way

And being warned in a dream not to return to Herod, they departed to their own country by another way. Matthew 2:12 (ESV)

The magi are part of Christmas manger scenes, but they didn't visit Jesus at the same time as the shepherds. They came much later to a house (Matthew 2:11).

Led by an unusually bright star, they traveled over the desert for many months, without modern transportation or fancy hotels, seeking the "King of the Jews." In Jerusalem, their inquiries attracted the concern of King Herod who "sent them to Bethlehem and said, 'Go and search carefully for the child. As soon as you find him, report to me, so that I too may go and worship him'" (2:8).

When the magi saw Jesus, they bowed down, worshiped him, and gave him gifts. Afterward, God warned them in a dream not to return to Herod. They went home by another way.

I've always wondered about that trip home. Did their visit with Jesus change their lives?

The first time Jesus became real to me was at a service where a call went out for missionaries. I found myself in tears and went to the altar even though I knew I wasn't called to be a missionary. When I told the leaders how I felt, they had me sit to one side and went off to speak to the others. They didn't realize I had responded to a call from God. Nothing seemed to change. I went home the same way.

I believe my spirit was reborn at that time. Years later, I discovered that God desired to commune with me regularly through prayer, the Bible, other Christians, books, and websites such as DigDeeperDevotions.com.

How about you? Has something you've read this Christmas stirred a desire to meet Jesus or have you recalled memories of an experience you had years ago? Has your life changed? Do you commune with him on a daily basis through prayer and Bible study?

Will you go into the new year by another way?

DIG DEEPER

1. Are you willing to journey wherever God leads to see the Son? Read John 3:6–21 and 6:37–39.

2. The gospel of John doesn't include the story of Christ's birth or the visit of the magi. John goes back much further. Read John 1:1–2, 10–14. What does he say about who Jesus is?

3. Read 2 Corinthians 4:6. How does God show himself to us?

4. Read Colossians 1:9–20. This is what I am praying for you. Who can you pray for?

December 31: The Ponder Anew Year

But Mary treasured up all these things and pondered them in her heart. Luke 2:19

The year had been extraordinary. Miraculous. As Mary cradled her newborn son in her arms, she pondered what had transpired in the previous twenty-four hours and perhaps everything else that had happened since the angel Gabriel appeared to her all those months ago.

Could this sleeping infant truly be the Son of the Most High, Jesus Christ the Lord? It must be so. Everything about Mary's year pointed to the truth of Gabriel's words: the angel's unexpected announcement, Joseph's gracious response to her pregnancy, Cousin Elizabeth's enthusiastic affirmation, and the shepherds' angelic encounter. Unbelievable, yes, but also undeniable. (Consider Matthew 1:18–25; Luke 1:39–45; Luke 2:15–20.)

So Mary pondered "all these things." The Greek word translated "ponder" in many translations is *symballo*: "to put one thing with another in considering circumstances."[15] English translators chose wisely when they selected *ponder*, derived from an Old French word that means "to weigh, to estimate the worth of, to appraise."[16]

How often do we weigh the worth of the Christmas story as it relates to our daily life? How does knowing that God became flesh to save me from my sins and give me eternal life influence the way I conduct business, choose leisure activities, spend money, and cultivate relationships?

More than 300 years ago, a German Latin teacher, Joachim Neander, pondered the evidence of God's mighty deeds in his life. He wrote these words:

> Praise to the Lord,
> who doth prosper thy work
> and defend thee;
> Surely His goodness and mercy
> here daily attend thee.
> Ponder anew what the Almighty can do,
> If with His love He befriend thee.

The Almighty God has befriended us. That's the essence of the Christmas story. And he showers us with goodness and mercy every day. What should our response be? Solomon phrased it this way: "Ponder the path of thy feet, and let all thy ways be established" (Proverbs 4:26 NKJV). Or, as another translation says, "Mark out a straight path for your feet; stay on the safe path" (NLT).

When we ponder anew what the Almighty has done and can do, we'll want to ponder the path of our feet. We'll want to stay on the safe, straight path marked out by God's Word. That's what Mary did. That's what Solomon and Neander encouraged us to do.

May this coming year be a "ponder anew" year for each of us. And may our pondering lead us ever closer to the One who loved us enough to become one of us—Jesus Christ the Lord.

DIG DEEPER

1. According to Proverbs 5:21, what does God ponder? (translated "examine" in the NIV). Does that comfort you or convict you? Maybe a little of both?

2. Read Psalm 77. What is the psalmist's mind-set at the beginning of the psalm? What does he ponder anew in verses 10–20? How do those remembrances change his mind-set? What do you ponder in troubling times?

3. Read 1 Samuel 12:19–25. What did Samuel encourage the Israelites to ponder ("consider" in the NIV) as they transitioned into a new political era under the leadership of a king? What was Samuel's warning? What advice might Samuel give us as we enter a new year?

"Praise to the Lord, the Almighty"

Joachim Neander, 1680
Translated into English by Catherine Winkworth, 1863
Public Domain

Praise to the Lord, the Almighty,
the King of creation!
O my soul, praise Him,
for He is thy health and salvation!
All ye who hear,
now to His temple draw near;
Praise Him in glad adoration.

Praise to the Lord, who over all things
so wondrously reigneth,
Shelters thee under His wings,
yea, so gently sustaineth!
Hast thou not seen
how thy desires ever have been
Granted in what He ordaineth?

Praise to the Lord,
who hath fearfully,
wondrously, made thee;
Health hath vouchsafed
and, when heedlessly falling,
hath stayed thee.
What need or grief
ever hath failed of relief?
Wings of His mercy did shade thee.

Praise to the Lord,
who doth prosper thy work
and defend thee;
Surely His goodness and mercy
here daily attend thee.
Ponder anew what the Almighty can do,

If with His love He befriend thee.

Praise to the Lord, who,
when tempests their warfare are waging,
Who, when the elements
madly around thee are raging,
Biddeth them cease,
turneth their fury to peace,
Whirlwinds and waters assuaging.

Praise to the Lord,
who, when darkness of sin is abounding,
Who, when the godless do triumph,
all virtue confounding,
Sheddeth His light,
chaseth the horrors of night,
Saints with His mercy surrounding.

Praise to the Lord,
O let all that is in me adore Him!
All that hath life and breath,
come now with praises before Him.
Let the Amen sound from His people again,
Gladly for aye we adore Him.

[1] "G2090 - hetoimazō - Strong's Greek Lexicon (KJV)." Blue Letter Bible. Accessed 11 Aug, 2017. https://www.blueletterbible.org//lang/lexicon/lexicon.cfm?Strongs=G2090&t=KJV.

[2] "H6437 - panah - Strong's Hebrew Lexicon (KJV)." Blue Letter Bible. Accessed 25 Sep, 2017. https://www.blueletterbible.org//lang/lexicon/lexicon.cfm?Strongs=H6437&t=KJV. See full explanation of panah under "Gesenius' Hebrew-Chaldee Lexicon."

[3] Babylonian-Canaanite goddess of fortune and happiness, the supposed consort of Baal from Dictionary and Word Search for 'asherah (Strong's 842)". Blue Letter Bible. 1996-2012. 22 Dec 2012. http://www.blueletterbible.org/lang/lexicon/lexicon.cfm?Strongs=H842&t=NASB.

[4] "H6923 - qadam - Strong's Hebrew Lexicon (NASB)." Blue Letter Bible. Accessed 11 Aug, 2017. https://www.blueletterbible.org//lang/Lexicon/Lexicon.cfm?Strongs=H6923&t=NASB.

[5] "G4692 - speudō - Strong's Greek Lexicon (NASB)." Blue Letter Bible. Accessed 11 Aug, 2017. https://www.blueletterbible.org//lang/lexicon/lexicon.cfm?Strongs=G4692&t=NASB.

[6] Charles Dickens, A Tale of Two Cities, 1859, Public domain.

[7] Hope. "Hebrew Lexicon :: H3176 (KJV)." Blue Letter Bible. Accessed 2 Nov, 2013. http://www.blueletterbible.org/lang/lexicon/lexicon.cfm?Strongs=H3176&t=KJV.

[8] Haggai 2:7 is also translated "they will come with the wealth of all nations" (NASB) or "the treasures of all nations shall come in" (ESV) instead of "what is desired by all nations will come" (NIV) or "the desire of all nations shall come" (KJV). However, all translators agree that the verse refers to the future reign of Jesus Christ.

[9] "H3467 - yasha` - Strong's Hebrew Lexicon (NIV)." Blue Letter Bible. Accessed 25 Sep, 2017.

https://www.blueletterbible.org//lang/lexicon/lexicon.cfm?Stron
gs=H3467&t=NIV.

[10] "H1350 - *ga'al* - Strong's Hebrew Lexicon (KJV)." Blue Letter
Bible. Accessed 12 Aug, 2017.
https://www.blueletterbible.org//lang/lexicon/lexicon.cfm?Stron
gs=H1350&t=KJV.

[11] Hymntime.com.
http://www.hymntime.com/tch/bio/m/o/n/montgomery_j.htm and
UMC Discipleship Ministries
https://www.umcdiscipleship.org/resources/history-of-hymns-
angels-from-the-realms-of-glory. Accessed 25 Sept, 2017.

[12] G3170 -- *megalyno* -- Greek Lexicon :: G3170 (KJV)." Blue
Letter Bible. Accessed 4 Nov, 2014.
http://www.blueletterbible.org/lang/lexicon/lexicon.cfm?Strongs
=G3170&t=KJV.

[13] *The Revell Bible Dictionary,* (Grand Rapids: Fleming H.
Revell, 1994), 588.

[14] "H3091 - *Yĕhowshuwa`* - Strong's Hebrew Lexicon (NKJV)."
Blue Letter Bible. Accessed 25 Sep, 2017.
https://www.blueletterbible.org//lang/lexicon/lexicon.cfm?Stron
gs=H3091&t=NKJV.

[15] Vine, W. "Dictionaries :: Ponder." Blue Letter Bible. Last
Modified 24 Jun, 1996.
http://www.blueletterbible.org/search/Dictionary/viewTopic.cfm.

[16] "Ponder." Etymonline.com,
http://etymonline.com/index.php?allowed_in_frame=0&search=
ponder&searchmode=none.

About the Authors

Nancy J. Baker is a writer, editor, and Bible teacher. She encourages biblical literacy using the Bible to interpret itself and making connections between the Old and New Testaments. At her church, Nancy co-leads women's Bible studies and has begun to present studies she has written, including *Seniors in Scripture.* She also leads a small group with her husband. They both have contributed to devotional booklets published by their church. Nancy creates quarterly biblical word search puzzles for *Power for Living.* She alternates with Denise Loock to write a new devotional Bible study weekly on digdeeperdevotions.com. For more info, visit digdeeperdevotions.com/about-Nancy. She and her husband, Ken, live in New Jersey.

Denise K. Loock is an editor, writer, and speaker. Through speaking engagements, books, and DigDeeperDevotions.com, she shares with others the joy of studying God's Word. As a book editor, she uses her twenty-nine years of experience as an English teacher to help Lighthouse Publishing of the Carolinas produce high quality, engaging inspirational fiction and nonfiction books. She also accepts freelance editing projects. She is the author of two devotional books that highlight the Scriptural truths of classic hymns and gospel songs, *Open Your Hymnal* and *Open Your Hymnal Again.* For more info, visit digdeeperdevotions.com/about-denise.

Contact her at denise@lightningeditingservices.com or info@digdeeperdevotions.com. She and her husband, Mace, live in North Carolina.

Dig Deeper Devotions is a website designed to encourage and enable you to dig deeper into God's Word on your own. Each devotion on the website takes an insightful look at a Scripture passage and provides a practical application. Then we suggest a few ways you can dig deeper into a word, a person, or a topic so you can develop the Bible study skills you need to grow as a Christian.

We don't publish a new devotion each day; we post a new featured devotion each week on Thursday or Friday. We encourage you to read the passages suggested in the Dig Deeper section and to use the study helps in your Bible to explore other Scriptures too.

Hundreds of devotions are available on the website. Explore them today: digdeeperdevotions.com.

To Our Readers

If you've enjoyed this collection of devotions, please consider writing a customer review on Amazon. We'd also love to hear from you. Contact us at info@digdeeperdevotions.com.

Coming February 1, 2019, is the release of our second Dig Deeper devotional collection, *Restore the Hope: Devotions for Lent and Easter*. For more information about this book, contact us at info@digdeeperdevotions.com.

Made in the USA
Columbia, SC
26 November 2023

26704822R00083